ADA
Guidelines
for Practice
Success™
(GPS™)

Managing Patients

The patient experience: best practices

ADA American Dental Association®
America's leading advocate for oral health

Acknowledgments

This publication was developed by the American Dental Association's Center for Dental Practice. The ADA thanks the following individuals for their contributions:

- *Dr. Joseph G. Unger, chair, Council on Dental Practice*
- *Dr. Jean L. Creasey, Council on Dental Practice*
- *Dr. J. Christopher Smith, Council on Dental Practice*
- *Dr. Irene Marron-Tarrazzi, New Dentist Committee*
- *Ms. Lois Banta*
- *Ms. Denise S. Ciardello*
- *Ms. Debra Engelhardt-Nash*
- *Ms. Linda Harvey*
- *Ms. Ginny Hegarty*
- *Ms. Judy Kay Mausolf*
- *Dr. Lillian Obucina*
- *Ms. Christine Taxin*
- *Dr. William van Dyk*

In addition to the individuals cited above, principal contributors to this publication include Dr. Pamela M. Porembski, director, Council On Dental Practice, Cynthia Kluck-Nygren, manager, Dental Teams Activities and Publications, and Dr. Diane Metrick, senior manager, Special Projects and Emerging Issues.

Table of Contents

Table of Contents

Introduction

Your ability to communicate with patients impacts their perception of your practice. Managing that perception is critical to providing patients with ethical, personalized, high-quality care that maintains, or improves, their oral health and their overall health and well-being. It's also an important factor in developing and fostering a trusting relationship based on mutual respect that can last for decades.

The Patient Experience: What It Is and Why It Matters

The best way to understand the importance of your patients' experience with your practice is to put yourself in their shoes. Consider these questions, not as a dentist, but as a patient:

- What would you want and expect from your dentist?
- What would you want and expect from the members of the dental team?
- What makes a dental visit a positive experience, even if the treatment or care provided involves discomfort?
- What makes you willing to return to the same practice?

Good communication is the cornerstone of any successful practice.

The answers to those questions can make a huge difference in your ability to develop positive relationships with your patients. When they are considered from both a personal and a business perspective, those answers can affect your no show, cancellation and case acceptance rates, patient referrals, and treatment plans.

Dental care has been driven by preventive and restorative treatment, and the foundation of every clinical procedure you recommend and perform is built on the relationship you've established with each patient. Like the team of dental professionals supporting you in providing care, your patients are part of your dental family. From the first phone call to the completion of the treatment plan, your ability to successfully communicate with patients will determine how effectively you meet their expectations. Good communication is the cornerstone of any successful practice.

The Managing Patients module of the American Dental Association's Guidelines for Practice Success™ (GPS™) details aspects of patient management via four major topics that offer a framework for handling some of the elements of communication that can make or break the patient experience.

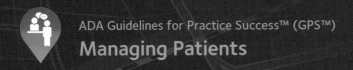
Patient Intake

Although everything your team has done up to this point is important, you really do have only one chance to make a first impression. Most new patients are very aware of what they see and hear the minute they open your front door. These tips can help you and your team make every patient feel welcome and confident in their selection of you as their dentist.

Phone Calls from Prospective Patients

Even though people are doing more from their computers, phones and tablets, a phone call is still likely to be the first communication with your practice. Follow these tips to make a patient's right connection:

- Try to answer every phone call by the third ring.

- The person who answers the phone should speak "with a smile" in his/her voice. Try it; having a smile on your face really does make your voice friendlier.

- Have a standard greeting that is used without exception by everyone who answers the phone. Make sure it mentions the name of the practice, the name of the person speaking and that it invites the caller to share the reason for their call.

- Use scripts to handle the most frequent topics covered over the phone, whether it's visiting the practice, changing or canceling an appointment, or handling an emergency, etc.

    ◦ Scripts ensure that the same message is communicated to every patient every time.

    ◦ Have your team role play different telephone scenarios so they become comfortable with them.

- Don't allow interruptions or put callers on hold unless there is a medical emergency or a situation that requires staff members to abandon their duties. Short holds to answer another line before the fourth ring may be necessary.

- Once callers indicate they're interested in a first appointment, restate your name and ask for theirs.

Scripts ensure that the same message is communicated to every patient every time.

Have your team **role play different telephone scenarios** so they become comfortable with them.

Managing Patients

- Start completing a new patient intake form.

  Basic questions that should be on the form include:

  ◦ The date of the caller's most recent dental appointment

  ◦ The patient's availability

  ◦ Any medical issues

  ◦ How they prefer to be contacted if necessary

  ◦ Whether they have coverage through a dental benefit plan

  ◦ Any other information that will allow you and your staff to better accommodate them

- Thank callers for contacting your practice and invite them to visit the office, even if they don't make an appointment. While few callers will take you up on the offer, it lets them know that your practice is an accessible and caring environment.

- Make sure every caller feels like he or she is the most important person you'll talk with all day.

- Have the front desk staff direct all new patients to the practice website. You and your staff can even suggest specific pages with content that's relevant to their visit. Of course, make sure your website looks professional, has strong visual appeal and is easy to navigate.

  ◦ Consider whether you're comfortable with patients making online appointments; if so, ask your webmaster if that feature can be integrated into your website.

  ◦ Many practices also offer a newsletter, available by an "opt-in" email and via the practice website. This is a great way to keep patients engaged with you and your practice.

Resources:

- **Standard Telephone Protocols**, p.5

- **Sample Phone Scripts**, p.6

- **Sample New Patient Intake Form**, p.9

Make sure every caller feels like he or she is the most important person you'll talk with all day.

Consider whether you're comfortable with patients making **online appointments;** if so, ask your webmaster if that feature can be integrated into your website.

Managing Patients

STANDARD TELEPHONE PROTOCOLS

- Smile each time you answer the phone. That simple act actually puts a pleasant, friendly and helpful tone in your voice. Always think of the person on the phone at the time as the most important person you will speak to that day.

- Always remember that your telephone style projects an image of the practice and can influence whether or not a prospective patient decides to become part of your practice.

  Make sure every caller feels valued and welcomed, whether they are a longtime patient, a prospective patient looking for a new dentist, or even a vendor or sales rep. Remember, new patient referrals can come from anywhere.

- Speak slowly, enunciate clearly.

- Always be calm, professional, respectful and project genuine concern. Concentrate on what the caller says, listen attentively without interrupting, confirm the situation (especially if it's an emergency), evaluate the urgency, and pass the information on with complete accuracy.

- Practice, or adapt, scripts so they sound natural and not forced or like you're reading from a page.

- Remember that no one likes to be put on hold, so do that only when absolutely necessary.

- If it's an emergency, try to make an appointment for the same day, regardless of whether the caller is a patient of record. A helpful, empathetic approach and a successful outcome can convert an emergency appointment into a long-term patient. If it's not possible to schedule the patient for the same day, explain the situation and refer the caller to a trusted colleague who is able to see the patient that day, or (if that is not available), suggest where the patient might be seen sooner.

Managing Patients

SAMPLE PHONE SCRIPTS

▶ **USE THIS LANGUAGE FOR ALL CALLS:**

Front Desk Staff: "Good [*morning/afternoon*]. Thank you for calling [*practice name*]. This is [*greeter's name*]. How may I [*we*] help you?"

The caller's response will determine what you say next.

▶ **USE THIS LANGUAGE FOR NEW, PROSPECTIVE PATIENTS:**

Front Desk Staff: "We appreciate your interest in our practice. How can we help you?"

▶ **USE THIS LANGUAGE IF THE PATIENT NEEDS IMMEDIATE OR EMERGENCY TREATMENT:**

Front Desk Staff: "I'm sorry that you're in pain. Let me see how soon Dr. [*insert name*] can see you. We'll do our best to get you in as soon as possible."

▶ **USE THIS LANGUAGE IF THE PATIENT IS A "TELEPHONE SHOPPER":**

Front Desk Staff: "Are you able to schedule a visit to our office? We'd like to show you the facilities and introduce you to the staff and the doctor(s). We can answer any questions you might have at that time. If you'd like, we can even schedule an initial appointment at the same time so the doctor can assess your needs and determine the best treatment for you."

▶ **USE THIS LANGUAGE IF THE CALLER ASKS ABOUT THE DENTIST'S PARTICIPATION IN A SPECIFIC DENTAL BENEFITS PLAN:**

Front Desk Staff: "Good morning, thank you for calling [*practice name*], Jane speaking. How may I help you today?"

Patient: "Do you accept my [*name of dental benefits plan*]?"

Front Desk Staff: "I would be happy to assist you. May I ask your name?"

Patient: "Ms. Doe."

▶ **IF YOU DO NOT PARTICIPATE IN THE PLAN:**

Front Desk Staff: "Thank you, Ms. Doe. Dr. Cook and her team are wonderful. [*If the practice has patients with the particular plan, add*] Several of Dr. Cook's patients have the same dental benefits plan as you. We are not a preferred provider with your plan but we will assist you in maximizing your dental benefit reimbursement. May I schedule an appointment for you?"

▶ **IF YOU ARE A PARTICIPATING PROVIDER:**

Front Desk Staff: "Thank you, Ms. Doe, Dr. Cook and her team are wonderful. We are a preferred provider with your plan and will assist you in maximizing your dental benefit reimbursement. [*If the practice has patients with the particular plan, add*] We have several patients with your plan who see Dr. Cook. May I schedule an appointment for you?"

▶ **USE THIS LANGUAGE IF THE CALLER ASKS ABOUT FEES FOR A CLEANING:**

Patient: "How much do you charge for a cleaning?"

Front Desk Staff: "I would be happy to answer your question. My name is Jane. May I have your name please?"

Patient: "Ms. Doe."

Front Desk Staff: "We have different types of cleanings in our office, depending on your oral health needs. The fees range from $_____ to $_____. We invite you to come in and meet Dr. Cook so she can examine your mouth and determine what type of cleaning is best for you."

▶ **USE THIS LANGUAGE IF THE CALLER ASKS ABOUT FEES FOR A CROWN:**

Patient: "Hello, how much do you charge for a crown?"

Front Desk Staff: "Good morning, thank you for calling [*practice name*]. My name is Jane. May I have your name please?"

Patient: "This is Ms. Doe."

Front Desk Staff: "The fee for a crown will vary from $_____ to $_____ based on your specific needs and the materials used. We understand that many patients are concerned about cost. May I schedule a consultation for you to meet Dr Cook, have her examine you and take any necessary X-rays? Then we can provide you with a specific fee for your treatment. We are happy to do this at no charge! When would you like to come in? I can fit you in today at _____."

▶ **USE THIS LANGUAGE IF THE CALLER ASKS ABOUT FEES FOR AN IMPLANT:**

Patient: "How much do you charge for an implant?"

Front Desk Staff: "I would be happy to discuss the fees for an implant. My name is Jane. May I have your name?"

Patient: "Ms. Doe."

Front Desk Staff: "Thank you, Ms. Doe. The fee for an implant will vary from $_____ to $_____ based on your specific needs and the materials used. We understand that many patients are concerned about cost. May I schedule a consultation for you to meet Dr Cook and have her examine you and take any necessary X-rays? Once we have that information, we can provide you with a specific fee for your treatment. We are happy to do this at no charge! When would you like to come in? I can fit you in today at _____."

Managing Patients

▶ **USE THIS LANGUAGE IF THE CALLER EXPRESSES CONCERN ABOUT FEES:**

Patient: "The fees are so high."

Front Desk Staff: "Thank you for sharing your feelings. In [*practice name*], we are proud to provide the best dental care we possibly can. The fees are based on the materials used, the time, skill and advanced technology used to provide you with the level of care you can expect from Dr. Cook and her staff."

Or

Front Desk Staff: "Dental treatment is an investment in your health. Perhaps I can assist you. We have several payment options available; may I review them with you to see which would works best for you?"

Or

Front Desk Staff: "Is it possible for you to stop in today or one day this week? We'd like to schedule an initial appointment so the doctor can assess your oral health needs and develop a customized treatment plan that fits your specific needs. We can discuss treatment costs once we know what your needs are. At the same time, we can review ways for you to fit the treatment you need in your budget. In the meantime, do you have any questions about the practice that I can answer briefly over the phone?"

▶ **USE THIS LANGUAGE TO SCHEDULE APPOINTMENTS FOR PATIENTS OF RECORD:**

Patient: "Good morning, Susie. It's Ms. Doe. I'd like to schedule an appointment."

Front Desk Staff: "Hello, Ms. Doe. How are you? How can I help you today?"

- For longstanding patients who honor regular appointments, respond to their request for an appointment with "Let me try to get you in as soon as possible." And work to get them into the practice as soon as the schedule allows.

- For patients of record who frequently cancel or miss appointments, respond with "I will try to get you in as soon as possible. The next available opening is [*insert a date and time convenient to the office*]. Are you available then?" Once they're scheduled, respond with "We'll contact you with a reminder of the appointment [*insert timeframe*]. We look forward to seeing you."

▶ **USE THIS LANGUAGE TO END CALLS:**

Front Desk Staff: "Thank you for calling us today, [*insert name*]. We'll see you [*restate appointment date and time and the reason for the appointment*]. Have a great day!"

SAMPLE NEW PATIENT INTAKE FORM

FOR OFFICE USE ONLY:

Date: _____

Patient name:_____

Parent or legal guardian's name: _____

Address: _____

Email: _____

Cell phone: _____ Home phone: _____ Work phone: _____

Contact Preference: ☐ Cell ☐ Text ☐ Home phone ☐ Work phone ☐ Email

How did you hear about our office?

☐ Referral ☐ Website ☐ Signage ☐ Coupon ☐ Other: _____

Referral Source: _____

Are you experiencing any dental problems or have any dental concerns?

☐ Pain? Where?_____ ☐ Constant? ☐ Occasional?

☐ Swelling? Where?_____

Are you under the care of a physician? ☐ Yes ☐ No

When was your last dental visit? _____ Are x-rays available? _____

Name of previous dentist: _____ Phone number: _____

Address: _____

Do you have a dental benefit plan? ☐ Yes ☐ No
  If Yes:

Member ID number: _____ Group number: _____

Name of policy holder: _____

Policy holder's relationship to the patient: _____

Date of birth:_____

Policy holder's employer: _____

Insurance company: _____

Address: _____

Phone number and/or insurance company website: _____

Managing Patients

Scheduled appointment date: _____

Verification of eligibility and benefits by: _____

    ☐ Electronic   ☐ Fax   ☐ Verbal

Verification scanned, saved or written in record date: _____

Maximum benefits/year: $_____

Deductible amount: $_____

Has deductible been met?   ☐ Yes   ☐ No

Does deductible apply to preventive services?   ☐ Yes   ☐ No

Determine frequency of preventive services:

    ☐ Twice per year

    ☐ Once every six 6 months

    ☐ Other: _____

Date of last radiographs: _____

Prior tooth loss restrictions: _____

Any other restrictions or limitations: _____

_____

Benefits remaining for benefit year: _____

Additional information: _____

_____

Office Hours and Time Management

Every patient deserves the best care you can offer. While it might be tempting to schedule as many patients as possible, the goal of effective time management is to achieve a workable balance between quality and quantity. While a full schedule may be appealing, over-scheduling could make you feel pressure to rush through appointments. The quantity of dentistry can never outweigh the quality. Compromising the quality of patient care could risk the viability of your practice.

Try to match your office hours to the times the majority of your patients are able to come in. Consider evening or weekend hours if an analysis of your patients' availability finds that many, if not most, need appointments during those hours.

- Consider your patients' demographics and availability when setting your office hours and schedule.

  ○ Offer evening and weekend appointments if possible to help schedule patients with limited availability.

- If patient demand warrants, you may want to consider adding an associate to the practice in order to accommodate patients' availability.

Open communication and a good working relationship with your team members who schedule appointments can keep patients moving in and out of the practice smoothly and at optimum production levels.

- Let your team members who schedule appointments know your preferences, such as whether you prefer to perform certain procedures on certain days of the week or at certain times of the day.

  ○ Keep in mind that this process requires time, constant feedback and flexibility. Both you and your team members who schedule appointments need to be willing to compromise.

  ○ Develop a plan for educating your team about how you want the schedule to flow and for resolving scheduling conflicts that might arise. Recognize that your team is working to balance your directions with patients' requests, which can sometimes be very insistent.

Offer **evening and weekend appointments** if possible to help schedule patients with limited availability.

Develop a plan for educating your team about how you want the schedule to flow and for resolving scheduling conflicts that might arise.

Managing Patients

- Determine how much daily practice time should be devoted to consultative, diagnostic and clinical work.

  - Work with your team members who schedule appointments to reinforce those goals and explain how following the plan contributes to better patient care and increased profitability.

- Leave time open daily for emergency appointments.

  - Many dentists allow a 30-minute window for emergencies.

  - Review your schedule each morning and talk with your team members who schedule appointments about the best time slot for emergency patients.

- Accept and acknowledge that unavoidable delays sometimes cause you to run behind schedule.

When that happens, your staff should apologize to any patients kept waiting. They should not offer a vague statement such as "the doctor is very busy." Your patients expect you to be busy. They're busy too, and they want their appointments kept in sync with their schedules. You should also offer an apology to any patient kept waiting more than a few minutes and consider mailing a letter of apology directly from the dentist to any patient who has had to wait more than 20 minutes recognizing the importance of their time. While it takes some time and effort, that patient will appreciate the extra effort and attention. It can also help overcome any frustration the patient may have experienced.

Review your schedule each morning and talk with your scheduler about the **best time slot for emergency patients**.

Reception Area and Office Décor

Your office décor communicates your attitude towards patients, your philosophy of dental practice, and maybe even a little about your interests outside of the practice. Since this is a new patient's first real contact with you, take a moment to see it through their eyes. Step outside, and before coming back in, imagine you're a new patient entering the practice for the first time. How does the front desk and reception room look? Is it clean, tidy and orderly? Are the color schemes and furnishings outdated or showing signs of wear? A cheery, pleasant and comfortable reception room will put patients at ease and offer subtle cues about how much you value your patients.

Your **office décor** communicates your attitude towards patients, your philosophy of dental practice, and maybe even a little about your interests outside of the practice.

Managing Patients

- You may want to consider whether the reception area is cheerful and comfortable without being obviously showy or extravagant.

- Remember that women make 85% of all health care appointments for their families. Make the reception area comfortable for them.

- Remember that patients may use what they see around them to form an opinion about the quality of care you provide. Make sure the reception area reflects the quality, cleanliness, and state of the art of your practice.

Resources:

- **Reception Area and Office Décor Checklist**, p.14

The Patient's First Visit

The patient's first visit to your practice sets the tone for the future of the relationship. A positive initial experience translates to a positive, long-term relationship. Remember that the new patient's first visit should always end with them being given a special welcome packet that includes the basics (toothbrush, toothpaste, floss, etc.) as well as any pamphlets, brochures, and other appropriate informational materials that relate to the patient's needs. Avoid materials that depict the less attractive side of dental work, e.g., blood.

A warm welcome puts patients at ease and makes them feel like they're part of your practice family. When you make the best first impression you can, patients will feel comfortable and confident that they're in the right place for their oral health care.

- Train your receptionist to use the new patient's name to greet them as soon as they arrive.

- Your front desk staff should welcome each patient with a smile, state his or her name, and ask the patient's name. Whenever possible, approach new patients before they get to the reception area and shake their hand.

Your front desk staff should **welcome each patient with a smile,** state his or her name, and ask the patient's name.

RECEPTION AREA AND OFFICE DÉCOR CHECKLIST

The reception area and office décor communicate your philosophy of dental practice and your attitude towards patients. It's the first physical contact your patients have with your practice and it leaves an all-important first impression. Everything from clutter to furniture in need of repair — or replacement — will impact the patient's perception of you, your staff and the quality of care that you provide.

The first and best way to evaluate your reception area and office décor is to enter the front door just as your patients would. Step out of the practice and enter it, viewing everything from the patient's perspective. The checklist below will help you determine which areas, if any, of your practice could use a little updating.

Is the reception area cheerful, comfortable and welcoming?

Is it tasteful without being showy, fancy or too trendy?

Does it make a positive impressive without making patients think that you're charging too much or that they won't be able to afford services?

It is neat and clean, without any visible clutter?

Are the furnishings modern, tasteful and comfortable?

Is the furniture in good condition without any visible signs of wear and tear?
Keep in mind that a reception area that's seen better days may cause patients to think that your techniques and equipment might be a little outdated too.

Is the temperature comfortable?

Can patients sit in any area without feeling any direct air flow?
Make sure it's comfortable throughout every season and not too hot, too cold, too muggy or too stale.

Do the pictures on the walls and any decorations on tables or counters match?

Is there a single, unified theme to the artwork?
Artwork or other visual elements are key to your décor. Some practices integrate tropical fish tanks (make sure they're clean and quiet) and others use textile art since it provides a calming visual effect and prevents echoes by absorbing sound. Make sure that whatever you use fits the décor of the practice and isn't too showy.

Is the background music soft and soothing?
Many practices play "smooth jazz" since its timeless sound appeals to most age groups and demographics. Practices that play a specific radio station should choose one that doesn't have a lot of commercial breaks or on-air talent that makes remarks that some might find offensive. You may want to consider subscribing to a service that provides the type of music that you want and takes care of any licensing and copyright arrangements for you as part of the agreement.

Managing Patients

Does your décor appeal to your primary patient population?

Practices with a mature patient base shouldn't have too many toys or children-oriented objects since adult patients may think that the majority of your patients are children and that you won't be knowledgeable about state-of-the-art treatments for adults.

Materials for children can be kept behind the reception desk and offered to children when they arrive. Appropriate materials include kids' magazines, drawing and coloring supplies, and books and puzzles.

If your practice has a mix of young and old patients, see if it's possible to have a separate room where children can play under the watchful eyes of their parents.

Are any reading materials current and age appropriate for your patient base?

Do they match the interests, demographics and age groups of your patients?

Are magazines arranged neatly?

Keep a variety of current magazines available on low tables or a rack/stand and have someone up front neaten them up several times each day. Provide magazines that promote general health and wellness in addition to those that promote special interests.

Is your diploma visible?

Do you display your certificates of membership in leading dental organizations?

Are any special awards or citations you've received visible for patients to see?

While you don't need a "Wall of Fame" that highlights every professional achievement, knowing where you went to school and a little more about your professional accomplishments can boost patients' confidence. It can also spark conversations that allow you and your patients to relate on non-dental topics, which goes a long way in boosting loyalty.

Having these plaques and certificates in a main area, rather than in a single operatory, ensures that every patient sees them.

Do you have an album or picture frames that highlight "before" and "after" pictures of successful treatments?

These images can promote treatments and services available through the practice without being a "hard sell." Make sure you have written authorization from patients in the pictures to take and share those images. A sample photo release is on page 45.

Are print copies of your current practice newsletter available?

Even though you may email the newsletter to patients, some may not open or "click through" the email to read it. Or they might plan to read it later and forget to go back to it.

Have you assigned someone on staff responsibility for monitoring the office décor and letting you know when something needs to be repaired or replaced?

Assign your office manager or receptionist responsibility for noticing patients' reactions to the reception area and take note of what catches their eye and what causes them to cringe. That person should periodically inspect the furnishings to see if anything needs to be cleaned, repaired or replaced. They should also assess areas beyond the office itself, such as the lobby and exterior of the building.

Patient Registration and Forms

Request the necessary insurance data and a photo identification when you provide the patient with the standard new patient forms, typically the health history form, a declaration of the practice's payment policy, the Health Insurance Portability and Accountability Act of 1996 (HIPAA) forms, etc. Even if your practice is paperless, new patients are generally required to complete the necessary forms either in paper format (for scanning) or electronically.

- While some federal regulations require certain forms and protocols, be sure you know, and follow, relevant state laws, rules and regulations. Each state has its own laws regarding patients' medical and dental histories. Your state dental association may be able to assist you with specifics.

  - Check your state dental practice act to make sure that your patient recordkeeping forms are accurate and up to date.

  - Even if your state law doesn't require it, keep a complete and up to date medical and dental history on each patient. Having current information will help as you proceed with treatment plans since you'll be aware of medical conditions and prescriptions that could impact treatment or recovery.

- The American Dental Association (ADA) offers a comprehensive, printable health history form that covers both medical and dental issues.

- The Health Insurance Portability and Accountability Act of 1996 (HIPAA) emphasizes patient privacy and the protection of patients' protected health information (PHI). Designed to protect and enhance patients' rights, HIPAA codifies what patient information you can and cannot distribute and how that sharing must be done. Any practice that transmits certain information electronically must be HIPAA-compliant.

  - HIPAA's privacy regulations apply to all types of communications about patients' PHI regardless of the format, be it electronic, hard copy (paper, films and other materials), or spoken. Additional HIPAA security regulations apply to the electronic transmittal of PHI.

  - HIPAA regulations are complex. You are required to train every member of your staff in the proper handling of health information in order to ensure that the regulations are followed and that patients' PHI is protected.

Check your state dental practice act to make sure that your patient recordkeeping forms are accurate and up to date.

Even if your state law doesn't require it, keep a complete and up to date **medical and dental history** on each patient.

Managing Patients

- Designate a member of your staff to serve as the practice's HIPAA officer. Doing so emphasizes the importance of adhering to the law and can ensure that nothing slips through the cracks.

- Electronic claims submission can be a trigger that prompts HIPAA reviews. Any practice that submits claims electronically, or outsources that function to an external billing service, should be aware of, and in compliance with, all applicable HIPAA regulations.

- *The ADA Practical Guide to HIPAA Compliance Privacy and Security Kit* can help you develop HIPAA privacy policies and procedures for your practice. It includes such topics as:

  - implementing appropriate written office policy and procedures

  - developing forms to implement your policy

  - preparing your Notice of Privacy Practices

  - providing and displaying copies of the Notice to patients

  - identifying business associates

- Information on HIPAA requirements is also available in *A Dentist's Guide to the Law: 228 Things Every Dentist Should Know*

Resources:

- **Reception Area ADA Health History Form S500 English, S501 Spanish**. To order call 800 947-4746 or visit adacatalog.org

- **ADA Children's Health History Form S707D English, S503D Spanish**. To order call 800 947-4746 or visit adacatalog.org

- **HIPAA Regulations,** www.HHS.gov

- ***The ADA Practical Guide to HIPAA Compliance Privacy and Security Kit***. To order call 800 947-4746 or visit adacatalog.org

- ***A Dentist's Guide to the Law: 228 Things Every Dentist Should Know.*** To order call 800 947-4746 or visit adacatalog.org

Electronic claims submission can be a trigger that prompts HIPAA reviews.

The ADA Practical Guide to HIPAA Compliance Privacy and Security Kit can help you develop HIPAA privacy policies and procedures for your practice.

Touring the Practice

If time allows, take patients on a tour of the practice before they are escorted back to the operatory. If time is tight, it's good to share some basic information about the practice and offer a more complete tour at the end of the appointment.

- Patients generally want to know how big the practice is, including the number of operatories and the number and types of staff members.

- Be sure to mention any new, cutting edge or special equipment and explain how it allows the team to provide better patient care. Having state of the art technology, such as a digital radiographic or an intraoral camera system, lets patients know your practice is modern and up-to-date. That can make them feel more confident about choosing you as their dentist.

- Point out the infection control area and let them know the practice is committed to ensuring the health and safety of every patient and every member of the team. Let them know that the office follows the recommendations of the U.S. Centers for Disease Control and Prevention (CDC), and whether any staff members have recently completed additional infection control training or have special certification in the field.

- Let patients know if your practice has any special amenities, such as access to movies, complimentary beverages, engaging reading materials, dental education information, headphones, etc. if they arrive early.

- Make sure your staff recognizes when a patient isn't interested in a comprehensive tour that includes sterilization and staff rooms. Briefly mentioning the purpose of those areas may be enough information in those cases.

- Be careful with a full tour since sterilization areas and staff lounges are working, busy environments. Make sure the areas are ready to be viewed by patients.

- Remember that HIPAA requires reasonable efforts to prevent incidental disclosures of patient information. Take steps to prevent a patient from seeing another patient's protected health information.

Be sure to mention any **new, cutting edge or special equipment** and explain how it allows the team to provide better patient care.

Be careful with a full tour since **sterilization areas** and staff lounges are working, busy environments.

Meeting the Doctor

Have a team member escort the patient to an operatory as soon as possible once the forms are completed and the tour is over.

- Once the patient is comfortable in the chair, have a team member describe what will be done during the appointment and how those activities help you take care of them. Many dental practices perform medical screenings (blood pressure, pulse, temperature) and may sometimes take photos before beginning actual dental evaluation and treatment.

  - Ask the patient if recent radiographs are available before taking new ones.

  - Consult the *Dental Radiographic Examinations: Recommendations for Patient Selection and Limiting Exposure,* which were revised by the ADA and the U.S. Department of Health and Human Services' Food and Drug Administration in 2012.

- Welcome the patient to the practice before the examination. This is especially important for the patient's first visit.

- Have a team member interview the patient and discuss any dental concerns before sharing that information with you.

- Review the patient's name, chart and primary dental concerns so you can address the patient by name as you smile, shake hands, and welcome them to your practice. Be relaxed, be sincere, be yourself.

- Keep in mind that many patients experience some degree of dental anxiety. What you say and how you say it matters. Non-verbal cues such as body language and gestures are important. A confident yet relaxed dentist can go a long way in relieving patients' anxiety.

- Patients will notice how you relate to the members of your team. Be sure you interact with them in a natural way that demonstrates your respect and admiration for their skills and dedication.

- If it's difficult for you to make small talk or meet new people, concentrate on trying to express how much you value improving patients' quality of life by providing quality dental care.

  - Communicating with patients makes some highly-introverted dentists so anxious that it affects their ability to speak. Certain relaxation techniques, such as deep breathing, can induce a sense of calm. Focusing on the patient's concerns also can help.

Welcome the patient to the practice before the examination. This is especially important for the patient's first visit.

Review the patient's name, chart and primary dental concerns so you can address the patient by name as you smile, shake hands, and welcome them to your practice. **Be relaxed, be sincere, be yourself.**

- Break the ice with a few simple, pleasant questions that are harmless and non-intrusive. Try to find something other than dentistry that you have in common. Follow remarks about that topic with dentally relevant questions based on the information the patient has shared with your team.

  - Ask "open" questions that require the patient to provide a more detailed response than a simple "yes" or "no." This type of question usually results in more specific information about them, their home dental regimen and their experience with previous treatment. An open question is "What are your daily dental habits?" while a closed question is "Do you brush after every meal?"

  - Ask follow-up, closed questions later in the discussion if you need more details. Summarize all of the information by paraphrasing it and repeating it. This technique, sometimes called active listening, shows you're a good listener and an empathetic health care professional.

  - Positive body language and non-verbal cues, such as a relaxed, yet erect, posture and strong eye contact, convey that you are a competent and caring professional. Even though your work requires you to get up close and personal with patients, remember to respect their personal space during conversation. Also remember to adjust either the patient's chair or your own to ensure that you and the patient are at eye level for any conversation; this can build trust and ease any apprehension the patient might be experiencing.

  - Use as little technical language as possible when discussing findings from the oral exam and radiographs. Short, positive sentences that are supported by visual aids can help patients understand a concept or their oral condition. Explain to the patient the value and purpose of certain procedures, especially X-rays or impressions. If your practice has an intraoral camera, use it to help patients understand what you see.

  - You and the members of your staff should try to strengthen the personal connection with the patient at each visit. Discussing a shared interest strengthens the bond and cements the patient to your practice.

Break the ice with a few simple, pleasant questions that are harmless and non-intrusive. Try to find something other than dentistry that you have in common.

Resources:

- **Dental Radiographic Examinations: Recommendations for Patient Selection and Limiting Exposure, 2012**
  http://www.ada.org/~/media/ADA/Member%20Center/FIles/Dental_Radiographic_Examinations_2012.ashx

Policies

Fair but firm office policies are critical to keeping your practice running smoothly and efficiently. Your front desk staff should share all relevant policies with new patients during the first appointment and answer any questions they might have.

Financial: Payment Options, Handling Dental Benefits

Most practices have policies that explain the methods of payment accepted. These can include flexible payment options from external, third party lenders, prepayment and courtesy payment arrangements, and other internal financial arrangements.

Patients will appreciate knowing whether your office accepts their dental benefit plan and how the claim will be processed. Most patients will not know their specific benefits. Checking online portals of dental benefit companies for verification of benefits, deductibles, covered procedures and plan exceptions will help the patient with their financial arrangements.

Resources:

· **Sample Financial Policy Statement**, p.22

Patients will appreciate knowing whether your office accepts their dental benefit plan and how the claim will be processed.

SAMPLE FINANCIAL POLICY STATEMENT

Payment for services, including deductibles and copayments, is due at the time of the service unless other arrangements have been made prior to treatment. Payments may be made using cash, check, or credit cards. Any arrangements for third-party financing must be made before starting treatment.

[*IF your practice accepts dental benefit plans*]: [*Practice name*] accepts most dental benefit plans. We are happy to submit the claims necessary to see that you receive your benefits. The insurance contract is an agreement between you and the insurance company. You are ultimately responsible for all charges. We cannot guarantee that any coverage estimated by your plan will be paid once a claim is filed.

In order to maximize your benefits and because plans differ from carrier to carrier, and from policy to policy, our office may refer you to your carrier or your employer's benefits coordinator for assistance in understanding your plan. Please note that dental insurance is intended to cover some but not all dental care costs, and not all services are covered by your plan. You are responsible for payment of all services regardless of the payable benefit.

Checks that are returned to our office from your financial institution are subject to a $_____ returned check fee.* This fee covers the processing fees that are charged to our office. We would be happy to discuss our charges and how they relate to your particular situation.

Please indicate your understanding and acceptance of these financial policies by signing below.

_____   _____
Patient's name   Date

_____   _____
Patient, guardian or guarantor signature   Date

_____   _____
Witness name   Date

* Consult your state's applicable laws and regulations for limitations regarding fee limitations and restrictions.

Managing Patients

Cancellations

Despite the best of intentions, patients sometimes have legitimate reasons to cancel appointments. A small percentage of patients might be more prone to cancel frequently — or just not show up. Since the best offense is a good defense, it's important to motivate patients to keep their appointments by stressing how regular oral health care can lead to good systemic health.

- Most practices have a very specific cancellation policy, which is especially helpful for patients who are prone to cancelling appointments.

  - Patients are more likely to keep appointments if they know and understand that you expect them to be there.

  - Designate a member of the team to speak with patients who habitually cancel their appointments. Have them use a brief "elevator speech" that cordially but firmly advises the patient that the time set aside for their appointment is part of a carefully planned schedule.

  - Display your appointment policy in a prominent place visible to all patients. Stress the policy's importance by making the sign big, but not obtrusive.

  - Include the policy in every new patient package and have patients sign it to confirm they've received the notice. Some practices have a staff member also sign the document as a witness that it was provided.

  - Consider implementing a policy that charges patients a fee if they cancel their appointment with less than 24 or 48 hours' notice. Apply the penalty judiciously; charging a fee can strain the relationship. Long time patients likely don't expect to be charged for changing their appointment. Patients who are prone to canceling for no valid reason might benefit from a "disincentive" that encourages them to keep their scheduled appointments.

  - Since some staff members may be uncomfortable telling patients they owe money for an appointment they didn't keep, provide staff with a sample script that makes it easier to explain this policy to patients.

  - The ADA Patient Bill of Rights and Responsibilities provides additional information and suggestions for communicating patients' obligations.

- Where circumstances warrant, consider rescheduling cancelled appointments four to six weeks out rather than immediately. This allows you to maintain the normal flow of your schedule and imposes a natural consequence for cancelling without being heavy handed.

Display your **appointment policy** in a prominent place visible to all patients. Stress the policy's importance by making the sign big, but not obtrusive.

Use your practice management software to track patients who frequently cancel their appointments and then talk with them about the importance of **keeping their regularly scheduled appointments**.

Managing Patients

- Use your practice management software to track patients who frequently cancel their appointments and then talk with them about the importance of keeping their regularly scheduled appointments.

  ◦ Consider adjusting patient appointment times based on each patient's dependability. One possibility is double-booking appointments for patients who routinely fail to show; this will require the practice to adapt if the patient does show up on time. Another option is to schedule patients who are frequently late 30 minutes before their actual appointment so they actually arrive on time. Keep in mind that your front desk staff may need to adjust other patients' appointments in those situations.

Resources:

- **ADA Patient Bill of Rights and Responsibilities**
  http://www.ada.org/~/media/ADA/About%20the%20ADA/Files/
  statements_ethics_patient_rights.ashx

- **Sample Policies and Scripts**, p. 25

Make sure that the informed consent process is carried out for every patient by **having an office policy in place** that is referenced and followed in every case.

Managing Patients

SAMPLE CANCELLATION OR RESCHEDULING POLICY

If you find that you must change your appointment, we require a minimum of 24 hours' notice so that we may make every effort to accommodate other patients. If proper notice is not received, a fee may be charged for every appointment cancelled.

SAMPLE LATE ARRIVAL POLICY

Your appointment was scheduled to allow for enough time to provide the best service for you. Patients who arrive for their appointments more than _____ minutes late may have to be rescheduled. If you need to be rescheduled, you may be charged a fee of $_____.

SAMPLE SCRIPTS

▶ **PATIENT RESCHEDULING WITH DOCTOR:**

Front Desk Staff: "Good morning. Dr. Cook's office, this is Jane speaking. How may I help you?"

Patient: "Hi this is Ms. Doe. I need to reschedule my appointment."

Front Desk Staff: "Good morning, Ms. Doe. Dr. Cook was so pleased to see you were coming in today for the [*treatment*]. Is there any possibility of changing your schedule to keep the time we have reserved for you?"

Or

Front Desk Staff: "Ms. Doe, Dr. Cook recommended you complete treatment as soon as possible. Is there any possibility of you keeping today's appointment? We do not have any opening for [*treatment*] until [*name the date of the next available appointment*]."

Or

Front Desk Staff: "I will speak with Dr. Cook and call you back shortly. Can I reach you at [*recite phone number from caller ID or patient record*]? (Return the call with an appointment that recently became available.)

Or

▶ **PATIENT RESCHEDULING WITH HYGIENIST:**

Front Desk Staff: "Ms. Doe, I am sorry you will not be able to keep your Saturday appointment with [*insert hygienist's name*]. The next opening with [*insert hygienist's name*] is not until [*insert date*]. Saturday appointments are very popular. Are you sure you cannot keep your appointment? Is there anything I can do to help you keep the appointment?"

Informed Consent/Refusal

Informed consent is the basis for every treatment you propose to and perform on patients. Dentists *must* obtain informed consent from each patient or from the patient's legal guardian or decision-maker. State laws impact whether consent can be verbal or written. For common simple procedures such as an evaluation or prophylaxis for a healthy individual, the act of sitting in the dental chair may be interpreted as implied or waived consent. This too, may vary by state law.

The concept of informed consent is actually based on the "assault and battery" doctrine of old common law which would not allow one individual to lay hands on another person without permission. Keep in mind that informed consent is a process, not just a signature on a form. Many dentists find informed consent and documenting refusal of treatment a complex subject and benefit from continuing education dedicated to the subject. Ask your liability carrier if it offers courses on informed consent.

Make sure that the informed consent process is carried out for every patient by having an **office policy** in place that is referenced and followed in every case.

- Make sure that the informed consent process is carried out for every patient by having an office policy in place that is referenced and followed in every case.

  - You can develop an informed consent form based on existing customized templates or you can create your own. Practices that develop their own informed consent form should consider having the document reviewed by an attorney licensed in your state. Your liability company may also have suggestions on what to include in your informed consent process and form.

  - Having a patient sign a consent form does not satisfy your legal duty to discuss proposed treatment with the patient. Failure to have that conversation is a breach of your moral responsibility to the patient and, in the event of a malpractice lawsuit, could even raise questions about whether you actually received informed consent.

- At some point in their career, all dentists have a patient who refuses to consent to treatment. It is the patient's right to refuse consent. When that happens, carefully document the refusal and inform the patient of the potential health issues involved because treatment was refused. Document the discussion, the reasons for the refusal and the patient's understanding of those issues in the chart or in an informed refusal form. If the patient will not sign an informed refusal form, it would be prudent to document your conversation in the patient record (e.g., patient verbalizes understanding of the treatment needs but has chosen to decline treatment until more dental benefits are available).

- If a patient refuses treatment, you must decide whether or not to keep them in your practice. There is no right or wrong decision and each decision carries its own risks.

  ○ Even though the patient may have a dismissive attitude toward what you believe is an important issue, you have the moral and ethical responsibility to inform the patient of the best treatment possible and to make sure that the patient understands the potential risks of not proceeding with recommended treatment. This can minimize your liability and you'll sleep better at night knowing you did the right thing.

  ○ If you choose to continue to treat the patient, you are committing to evaluating and treating the patient for as long as the doctor-patient relationships exists. This means that you should continually inform the patient of the recommended treatment, even though it was previously declined, and to advise the patient of how the refused treatment can impact their oral health.

  ○ Informed refusal may indicate that you and the patient have different values and expectations. Consider whether it would be best if that patient is dismissed from the practice and referred to another dentist. Example: the patient who refuses a radiograph you believe essential to proper diagnosis and treatment. Information on dismissing a patient from the practice may be found in the "Patient Relations" section of this module.

Resources:

- **Sample Informed Consent Form**, p.29

- **Sample Informed Refusal Form**, p.30

If a patient refuses treatment, you must decide whether or not to keep them in your practice. There is no right or wrong decision and each decision carries its own risks.

INFORMED CONSENT

Informed consent is something a dentist should obtain from each patient or from the patient's legal decision maker, such as a parent or guardian, prior to treatment. It is more than simply having a patient sign a form.

Informed consent will differ based on diagnosis, proposed treatment options and state specific requirements. It includes a discussion with the patient of the nature of the proposed treatment, reasonable alternate treatment options, and the benefits and risks of each treatment. The patient should be advised of the time involved and cost of treatment, with written documentation in the patient's record detailing the discussion and that the patient understands, agrees with, and authorizes the treatment plan giving the dentist permission to proceed with treatment.

Your state dental society, legal counsel and your liability carrier may have information specific to your state.

Managing Patients

SAMPLE INFORMED CONSENT FORM

Patient name: _____ Date: _____

Treatment recommendations: _____

The benefit of recommended treatment: _____

Risks and possible complications: _____

Approximate duration of treatment phases: _____

Estimated cost of treatment: _____

Alternate treatment recommendations: _____

Risks and possible complications of alternative treatment: _____

[Patient name] I have reviewed and discussed the recommended treatments and alternative treatment recommendations with Dr. _____. I understand that no dental treatment is risk free, the risks have been explained to me and that the dentist will take reasonable steps to limit any complications. Dr. _____ has answered my questions about my treatment.

I have provided an accurate and complete medical history including medications I am taking and any known allergies.

I wish to proceed with the treatment recommendations.

Patient signature: _____ Date: _____

Dentist signature: _____ Date: _____

Witness signature: _____ Date: _____

© ADA 2015. Reproduction of this material by ADA member dentists and their staff is permitted. Any other use, duplication or distribution by any other party requires the prior written approval of the American Dental Association. **This material is educational only, does not constitute legal advice, and may not satisfy applicable state law. Changes in applicable laws or regulations may require revision. Contact a qualified lawyer or professional for legal or professional advice.**

SAMPLE INFORMED REFUSAL FORM

Patient name: _____ Date: _____

Treatment recommendations: _____

The benefit of recommended treatment: _____

The prognosis of the treatment (risks and possible complications): _____

Approximate duration of treatment phases: _____

Estimated cost of treatment: _____

Alternate treatment recommendations: _____

I am provided with this refusal form and information so I may understand the recommended treatment and the consequences of refusing treatment. I have had an opportunity to discuss and ask questions concerning the recommendations and alternative treatment recommendations.

The risks and complications to my oral and overall health have been explained to me if I do not proceed with the recommended treatment.

Complications include: _____

I have received the proposed treatment recommendations with the risks and complication information. I understand the recommendations and risks related to refusal of care.

Patient signature: _____ Date: _____

Dentist signature: _____ Date: _____

Witness signature: _____ Date: _____

Managing Patients

Specialty Referrals

Appropriate referrals to other providers are occasionally necessary in order to do what's best for your patients. Only you can assess whether your education, training, interest, and experience can provide the treatment needed by a particular patient. Cases that require referral to a specialist or another dentist with a specific skill set require clear, open and ongoing communication between providers and with the patient. Maintaining that communication allows you to effectively manage the patient's overall treatment and general well being, even from a distance.

- Discuss any proposed referral for treatment with patients right away so they can be active participants in determining their course of treatment.

- Patients may need to be referred for any number of reasons. Acknowledge and accept that no single provider can do everything.

  ○ In these cases, your patients need to understand that, while you are a highly-educated, trained and skilled dentist, their care can best be delivered by another dentist with more experience in a specific area. Explain, without going into unnecessary details, why you're recommending that treatment be done by another provider.

  ○ Reassure them that this transfer in providers is temporary, that you are still in charge of their care, and will be looking out for them. Soothe their doubts by discussing the education and credentials of the dentist to whom you are referring and let them know that you have complete confidence in the provider's training and expertise. Let them know you appreciate their trust in you, your professional judgment and treatment, and that you look forward to their return to your practice once this treatment is complete.

  ○ Be sure to explain:

    ▸ which area of dentistry or specialty was chosen and why

    ▸ whether they should make the initial appointment with the other dentist or if your staff will assist in making that first connection

    ▸ information about the specialist or consulting dentist's fee for the consultation or evaluation

    ▸ instructions that will make the patient's introduction to the specialist or consulting dentist a smoother transition. This could include preoperative instructions, educational pamphlets or even a map with directions.

Despite any discomfort you might feel, **the patient's oral health** and well being always take precedence.

Managing Patients

- Consult the ADA's General Guidelines for Referring Patients if you have any doubts or concerns regarding how to refer a patient for treatment.

- Dentists who are new to practice or new to a community may have a limited network of providers to whom they can refer. In those cases, reach out to connections from dental school, mentors, the local dental society, and your own knowledge of widely-respected specialists in individual disciplines to find the right referral.

- Sometimes dentists receive referred cases, or returned cases, in which it appears the patient has not received proper care. Do not discuss your concerns with the patient. Instead, reach out to the dentist who provided treatment and share your specific concerns in a matter-of-fact, non-accusatory, manner. In some cases, you may want to consider referring the patient to someone else for treatment. Despite any discomfort you might feel, the patient's oral health and well being always take precedence. You have a responsibility to make that difficult call when you feel one of your patients is not in the best hands.

- If an insurance carrier (third party payer) requests a second opinion from you regarding another dentist's diagnosis and treatment plan, which would result in a referral, you should conduct the case review in accordance with the ADA's Principles of Ethics and Code of Professional Conduct.

- Patients who present with complicated medical conditions may need an evaluation from their physician before dental care can be provided.

Consult the **ADA's General Guidelines** for Referring Patients if you have any doubts or concerns regarding how to refer a patient for treatment.

Resources:

- **ADA's General Guidelines for Referring Patients**
  https://success.ada.org/en/practice/operations/efficient-systems/general-guidelines-for-referring-dental-patients

- **ADA Principles of Ethics and Code of Professional Conduct**
  http://www.ada.org/en/about-the-ada/principles-of-ethics-code-of-professional-conduct

- **Sample Referral to Dental Specialist Form**, p.33

- **Sample Referral to Physician — Adult Form**, p.35

- **Sample Referral to Physician — Child Form**, p.37

Referral to Dental Specialist

Practice Name
Practice Address
Practice Phone Number

SPECIALTY REFERRAL TO: _____

Introducing: _____

Parent/Guardian: _____

Date of birth: _____

Address: _____

_____

Telephone: _____

REFERRED BY DOCTOR: _____

REASON FOR REFERRAL:　☐ Consultation　☐ Treatment

(Please provide specialist with appropriate details of problem; i.e. urgency, areas of concern.)

_____

RELEVANT HISTORY:
(Indicate any special factors — either dental or medical — such as known allergies and specific medical problems relevant to diagnosis and treatment.)

_____

_____

_____

_____

An appointment has been made: _____

Call referring doctor before treatment:　☐ Yes　☐ No

Radiographs:　☐ sent with patient　☐ none available

☐ Please provide written report.

Signed: _____　Date: _____

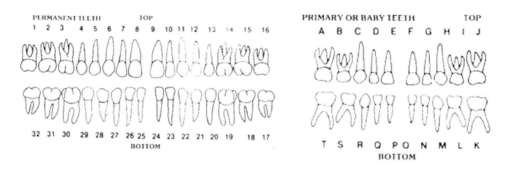

Referral for Medical Care (Adult)

From: Dr. [Name] DDS/DMD
          Practice Name (if applicable)
          Dr. Street Address
          Dr. City, state, zip
          Dr. Telephone/fax number
          Dr. Email address

To: Dr. [Name] MD/DO
     Dr. Street Address
     Dr. City, state, zip
     Dr. Telephone/fax number
     Dr. Email address

Date: _____ ☐ Urgent Care ☐ Routine Care

We are referring:

Patient name: _____

Date of birth: _____ Gender: ☐ Male ☐ Female

Street address: _____

City/State/Zip Code: _____

Cell phone: _____ Home phone: _____ Work phone: _____

Language spoken at home: ☐ English ☐ Other preferred language: _____

Appointment:

☐ Appointment scheduled on: _____ at: _____ AM/PM

Reason for Referral: *(check all that apply)*

☐ Medical evaluation related to the following (prior to dental treatment)

    ☐ coagulation issues   ☐ respiratory issues
    ☐ risk of seizures   ☐ anesthesia tolerance
    ☐ risk of CV incident
    ☐ other: _____

☐ Signs/symptoms of disease/condition. Describe: _____

☐ Evaluation of allergic reaction to: _____

☐ Routine medical care: _____

☐ Other: _____

Relevant History: *(check all that apply)*

☐ Dental problems: _____

    ☐ periodontal disease   ☐ cavities (caries)

    ☐ other: _____

☐ Special health care needs: _____

☐ Medications: _____

☐ Other: _____

Preferred Follow Up:

☐ Written or faxed report   ☐ None necessary

Referred by:

Name (Print): _____

Signature: _____

REFERRAL for Medical Care (Child)

From: Dr. [Name] DDS/DMD   To: Dr. [Name] MD/DO
           Practice Name (if applicable)   Dr. Street Address
           Dr. Street Address   Dr. City, state, zip
           Dr. City, state, zip   Dr. Telephone/fax number
           Dr. Telephone/fax number   Dr. Email address
           Dr. Email address

Date: _____   ☐ Urgent care   ☐ Routine care

We are referring:

Patient name: _____

Date of birth: _____   Gender: ☐ Male   ☐ Female

Parent/Guardian: _____

Street address: _____

City/State/Zip Code: _____

Cell phone: _____ Home phone: _____ Work phone: _____

Language spoken at home: ☐ English   ☐ Other preferred language: _____

Appointment:

☐ Appointment scheduled on : _____ at: _____AM/PM

☐ Parent/Guardian will call for appointment

Reason for Referral: *(check all that apply)*

☐ Medical evaluation related to the following (prior to dental treatment)

☐ Immunization record

☐ Evaluation for systemic disease

☐ Evaluation of allergic reaction to: _____

☐ Establish medical home; routine medical care: _____

☐ Other: _____

Relevant History: *(check all that apply)*

☐ Known allergies: _____

☐ Dental problems: _____

☐ Special health care needs: _____

☐ Medications: _____

☐ Other: _____

Preferred Follow Up:

☐ Written or faxed report   ☐ None necessary

Referred by:

Name (Print): _____

Signature: _____

Referral for Dental Care

From: Name: _____ To: Name: _____

          Address: _____   Address: _____

          City, State, Zip: _____   City, State, Zip: _____

          Phone/Fax: _____   Phone/Fax: _____

          Email: _____   Email: _____

Date: _____   ☐ Urgent care   ☐ Routine care

We are referring:

Patient name: _____

Date of birth: _____   Gender: ☐ Male   ☐ Female

Parent/Guardian (if applicable): _____

Street address: _____

City/State/Zip Code: _____

Cell phone: _____ Home phone: _____ Work phone: _____

Language spoken at home: ☐ English ☐ Other preferred language: _____

Appointment:

☐ Appointment scheduled on : _____ at: _____AM/PM

☐ Patient/Parent/Guardian will call for appointment

Reason for Referral: (check all that apply)

☐ Dental pain, facial swelling, dental trauma or other acute condition
   Describe: _____

☐ Evidence of dental disease present

☐ High risk for cavities

☐ Establish dental home; routine dental care

☐ Other: _____

Managing Patients

Relevant History: *(check all that apply)*

☐ Allergies: _____

☐ Medical problems: _____

☐ Special health care needs: _____

☐ Medications: _____

☐ Other: _____

Is premedication for dental treatment required?   ☐ No   ☐ Yes

Preferred Follow Up:

☐ Written or faxed report   ☐ None necessary

Referred by:

Name (Print): _____

Signature: _____

Miscellaneous Policies

- While constant and instant communication can be important, it's okay to ask patients to turn off or silence their cell phones and mobile devices during treatment since they can be distracting.

- If your practice has determined that cell phones and other mobile recording or photographic devices pose a risk to patient privacy, explain any restrictions to the patient.

General office policies about staff expectations and behaviors can play an important role in managing patients. While specific information will be developed in the guidelines relating to Managing the Dental Team (to be issued in 2016), it's important to keep the following points in mind:

- Delegate select policy-related duties to certain staff members based on what is allowed under your state's dental practice act. Team members should review the policy and sign and date a statement confirming that they've read it.

Dental office policies for staff frequently discuss the practice's:

- mission statement, e.g., "this dental practice exists to provide quality dental care to its patients on a timely and efficient basis."

- contact with patients and the public, e.g. "this office expects every employee to display good judgment, diplomacy, and courtesy when dealing with patients and the public, and to adhere to the highest standards of personal and professional ethics."

- policies on access to confidential information, telephone usage, appearance, receiving guests and visitors and performance of work.

Resources:

- *The ADA Practical Guide to Creating and Updating an Employee Policy Manual*, J670. To order, call 800-947-4746 or visit adacatalog.org

It's okay to ask patients to turn off or silence their **cell phones and mobile devices** during treatment.

Notes:

Treatment Recommendations

Case Presentations

The success of any dental practice is directly related to patients' acceptance of the dentist's treatment recommendations. A "choreographed" case presentation that blends spoken words with non-verbal cues and visual aids can increase patients' acceptance of your recommendations. In some cases, it can be helpful to support your case presentation with photographic images so the patient can see the condition being treated; make sure to have a signed photography release before taking, using or otherwise sharing those images.

- Make sure that your case presentations are clear, easy to understand and communicated in layman's terms.

  - Be sure that the patient is involved in the treatment decisions and that patient autonomy is respected.

  - Discuss the reason treatment is recommended, what to expect during and after treatment, and the risks associated with accepting-and not accepting-the recommended care.

  - Speak calmly, reassure patients that they'll be taken care of throughout the process, and encourage them to ask questions.

  - Explain what you are going to do and why. Step by step, say what will be done and why it needs to be done. Remind the patient throughout the discussion of the treatment benefits.

  - Present information in bite-sized pieces, perhaps breaking the treatment down by quadrant. Remember, you are communicating highly technical information to an anxious layperson.

The success of any dental practice is directly related to patients' acceptance of the **dentist's treatment recommendations**.

Managing Patients

○ Use as little technical language as possible. Rather than admit they don't understand what you're suggesting, many patients will conjure a simplified — and often distorted-translation that could scare them away from a procedure.

○ Speak in short sentences. One idea per sentence is easier to understand than a barrage of complex ideas coming at a patient in sentences a mile long.

○ Whenever possible, support your recommendations with visual aids, such as pictures, diagrams or ADA brochures that add clarity and more detail.

○ Deliver the case presentation in the context of a natural conversation, not a sales pitch.

○ Some patients may be nervous about treatment or worried about whether they can afford it. Let them know your practice has plans in place to help finance care and that your staff person (e.g., financial coordinator, office manager) will discuss those options with them.

· Case presentations for minor restorative treatment usually take place in the operatory. Use a private consultation room or your office to discuss major restorative work. The latter also applies to sensitive patients or those needing multiple appointments that will involve higher than average treatment costs.

Resources:

· **Sample Photography Release Form**, p.45

· **The Chairside Instructor: A Visual Guide to Case Presentations**, W013. To order call 800-947-4746 or visit adacatalog.org.

· Visit adacatalog.org to check out **ADA patient education brochures** on over 50 dental topics.

Case presentatio
for minor restorati
treatment usually
take place in the
operatory. Use a
private consultatio
room or your offic
to discuss major
restorative work.

SAMPLE PHOTOGRAPHY RELEASE FORM

I _____ the undersigned, do hereby authorize and consent to the use of photographs/X-rays of me taken by [insert dental office name]. I grant them permission to reproduce, print and publish photographs taken of me in a professional publication or in the form of prints, film or slides in connection with articles and lectures dealing with the jaw or dental disorders. I specifically waive any claim for invasion of my personal privacy which might accrue to me on account of the use of such pictures without my express consent in each instance.

I do consent to the use of my photographs or images for marketing materials including website and patient education for _____ [*name of practice*] only. I further understand that if the photographs and/or images are used, my name or similar identifying information will not be used.

No full face or comparable photos will be used without my express written authorization.

I further acknowledge that my participation is voluntary and that I will not receive any compensation, financial or otherwise, with respect to the taking, use or publication of these photographs for any dental office publications. I acknowledge and agree that publication of photographs confers no rights of ownership or royalties whatsoever.

Patient's name: _____

Patient's or guardian's signature: _____

Dentist's signature: _____ Date: _____

Street address: _____

City: _____ State: _____ Zip: _____

[Dental Office Name]
[Office address]
[Office city, state, zip code]

Managing Patients

Accepted Treatment

Ideally, patients who need more extensive treatment should return to the practice within one week for an appointment to discuss treatment options. Patients who have already made that first appointment are motivated to proceed with the care they need.

If too much time goes by before they are reappointed, it is less likely that they will come back, even when the treatment is necessary to restore their oral health.

- Have the patient sign the treatment plan. That document indicates the patient understands what you're recommending and why. It does not obligate them to proceed with treatment.

- Once the patient agrees to treatment, your documenter (financial coordinator/treatment coordinator/business assistant) should go over the financial details with the patient in private, such as in a consult room. This discussion should not take place while the patient is in the dental chair because it is often a stressful situation. Some states may have specific rules regarding the manner and privacy of financial discussions; refer to your state's laws for specifics.

Ideally, patients who need more **extensive treatme** should return to the practice within one week for an appointment to discuss treatment options.

Managing Patients

Emergency Treatment

The dentist must be available for patients of record anytime an emergency occurs, no matter when that might be. It's up to you to assess whether the situation is a true emergency or something that can easily wait until the next morning or when the practice reopens on the next business day. Keep in mind that patients in pain need to be reassured and offered relief from their symptoms.

- The voice mail message used when the office is closed should clearly advise callers with a life threatening emergency to dial 911 or immediately go to the emergency department of the nearest hospital. While that's typically not the case for dental issues, it's best to err on the side of caution.

  - The voice mail message should provide patients of record with an after-hours phone number they can call to reach you, such as "If you are an existing patient and this is a dental emergency, please contact Dr. Smith at (phone number)."

  - The voice mail message should also include emergency information for individuals who are not patients of record.

- Your office should have a defined contingency plan for handling emergencies and how to handle or refer patients if you are incapacitated. The ADA's *Guidelines for the Development of Mutual Aid Agreements in Dentistry* is one resource for handling these types of situations.

- Your office should be prepared to provide referral information to individuals who are not patients of record but who do contact you for emergencies.

- If your practice is busy, allow time in the schedule for emergencies. If your schedule is light, identify the best time to see emergency patients during your morning staff meeting.

- Your staff should also be trained in basic triage.

Resources:

- **Guidelines for the Development of Mutual Aid Agreements in Dentistry**
  http://ebusiness.ada.org/productcatalog/2270/Center-for-Professional-Success/Flexible-Benefit-Plans/CPS_PRO28

- **Sample Triage Reference Form for Front Desk Staff**, p.48

Keep in mind that patients in pain need to be reassured and offered **relief from their symptoms**.

SAMPLE TRIAGE REFERENCE FORM FOR FRONT DESK STAFF

*FOR OFFICE USE ONLY:

Completed by: _____

Patient name: _____

Date: _____ Time: _____

Contact number: _____

Appointment: _____

Schedule the patient <u>today</u> if they have any of the following acute symptoms:
- Recent trauma
- Avulsed tooth
- Fractured tooth
- Loose tooth
- Fever
- Swelling
- Sleep interruption from pain
- Persistent pain
- Post-surgical bleeding or complication
- Persistent reaction pressure and temperature
- Under physician care or referred by emergency room
- Fractured denture, not functional, unable to eat

Schedule the patient within <u>1-2</u> days if they have any of the following urgent symptoms:
- Lost or broken filling with minor or no discomfort
- No sleep interruption
- Minor discomfort relieved with over the counter (OTC) medications
- Minor or intermittent bleeding
- Occasional or intermittent discomfort
- Minor denture repair, functional

Schedule the patient at the first available appointment or within 1 week if they report:
- Occasional discomfort for several months
- Chipped or broken filling with no discomfort
- Discomfort responds to OTC medications
- Patient states not urgent
- Irritation or mild sensitivity
- Occasional sensitivity to cold

* Note: If patient can be identified from this information, include this document in your HIPAA compliance program.

Managing Patients

Post Treatment and Follow-up

You are partners with the patient in their post-treatment care. It's important for you to make sure that the patient understands their role and responsibilities following each appointment.

- It may be necessary to provide patients with written post-procedure instructions following certain treatments.

- Patients who have had extensive work done appreciate a follow-up phone call from their dentist to find out how they're feeling and to answer any questions.

It may be necessary to provide patients with **written post-procedure instructions** following certain treatments.

Recare Appointments

Most practice management software systems allow you to track appointments. It's important to contact patients to schedule recare appointments at the appropriate intervals for continuation of care. Keep in mind that some patients will prefer to make their next appointment at the end of the current one.

There are some patients that will not schedule recare appointments. Systems should be in place to track and engage these patients to keep them active in their healthcare prevention. One tip would be to utilize your practice management software program to run monthly reports of overdue patients and to designate a team member to contact them. With the proper office systems in place, office productivity and efficiency will increase.

- Recare appointments are essential to maintaining and monitoring patients' oral health. Pre-appointing hygiene patients at the end of their current appointment is a very efficient and productive strategy for recare.

- This is an opportunity for you to become a preventive health partner and build life-long relationships with your patients. Teach patients that regular visits to the dentist do not just maintain oral health, but may also help prevent serious health conditions and maintain optimal overall wellbeing.

- If the appointment is not added to a patient's calendar months in advance, they are likely to put it off indefinitely. With today's technology we are able to schedule appointments and issue pop-up reminders days, and even minutes, before the appointment is scheduled.

Pre-appointing hygiene patients at the end of their current appointment is a very efficient and productive strategy for recare.

Documentation/Patient Records

Patient records are a vital part of your practice. Among other things, they contain information about the patient's treatment plan and care that has been delivered. Dental records are especially important when submitting dental benefit claims or responding to lawsuits. While the dental record could be viewed as a form of insurance for your practice, make sure you include only those facts that are relevant to providing dental care. Follow the record keeping format you establish stringently and always keep in mind that what you write in the record could be read aloud in a court of law. After all, the patient record is a legal document.

- Whomever performs the treatment should document it in the record. All entries should be initialed or signed even if you are the only person who makes an entry in the patient record.

- You, the dentist, are responsible for the codes selected and documented in the patient record and billing systems. No matter who enters the information, you must make sure all of the information, including any procedure codes referenced, is correct.

Whomever performs the treatment should document it in the record.

Information typically noted in the dental record includes:

- personal data, such as the patient's name, date of birth, address and contact information including home, work and mobile telephone numbers

- the patient's place of employment

- medical and dental histories, notes and updates

- progress and treatment notes

- recaps of conversations about the nature of any proposed treatment, the potential benefits and risks associated with that treatment, any alternatives to the treatment proposed, and the potential risks and benefits of alternative treatment, including no treatment. Include conversations that took place in the office, over the phone and even calls received outside the office. Make sure that the recaps are dated and initialed.

- diagnostic records, including charts and study models

- medication prescriptions, including types, dose, amount, directions for use and number of refills

- radiographs

- photographs

- intraoral photographs

- treatment plan notes

- patient complaints and resolutions

- referral letters and consultations with referring or referral dentists and/or physicians

- patient noncompliance and missed appointment notes

- follow-up and periodic visit records

- postoperative or home instructions, or a notation about any pamphlets or reference materials provided

- informed consent/refusal forms

- waivers and authorizations

- correspondence, including a dismissal letter; if appropriate

- Information that should not be noted in the dental record includes:

  - any financial information, including ledger cards, insurance benefit breakdowns, insurance claims, and payment vouchers. The patient's financial records are not part of the clinical record and should be maintained separately.

  - personal opinions or criticisms. While it is okay to document a patient's refusal to accept the recommended treatment plan and information about cancelled appointments, be aware that disparaging comments and even informal notes written in the margins of a patient's chart must be shared if a lawsuit is filed.

  - keep patients' personal information in a location separate from their medical and dental records. Collecting that information on a separate form will make it easier to maintain separate files. Encourage team members to note each patient's special interests, hobbies and activities on that form.

Keep patients' **personal information** in a location separate from their medical and dental records.

Managing Patients

- Audit your dental records on a regular basis.

  ○ Auditing charts ensures that your records match those maintained by insurance companies, which often review a certain number of charts based on how many of their covered patients you've seen.

  ○ Audits allow you to confirm that patients have signed off on treatment plans and confirm that any changes in care from the original plan were discussed and approved.

  ○ Conduct clinical audits over time. This can serve as a quality assurance process that gives you direction for tweaking practice systems to improve operations. It can also facilitate brainstorming within the practice to avoid mistakes in the future.

- Announce all changes in the protocols or processes for maintaining patient records during staff meetings. Assign a staff member to take notes of the discussion so there's an official record of what specific changes were communicated, when they were communicated and to whom.

- Add a review of charts to the steps detailed on your close of the day sheet and follow each of the steps outlined.

  ○ Make sure everything was billed out correctly and completely.

Resources:

- **The ADA Dental Records 2010**
  https://success.ada.org/en/practice/operations/regulatory/dental-records

Announce all changes in the protocols or processes for maintaining patient records during staff meetings.

Appointment Confirmations

Many practices confirm patient appointments via text, email or phone at least one day in advance of the scheduled treatment. Talk with your staff about what method and timeframe works best for your patient base.

- Appointment reminders can be handled via telephone, email or smartphone texts. Ask patients to consent to the method of contact they prefer and make a note to handle all future appointment reminders that way.

  ○ Review HIPAA and make sure your practice complies with patient privacy regulations.

  ○ Use email only at the specific request of the patient.

  ○ Most dentists find that the standard practice of confirming appointments via telephone is still the most effective and efficient approach. Phone calls come with a friendly and familiar voice. That personal connection, which is missing from texts and email messages, makes it more likely the patient will keep the appointment.

  ○ Ask patients who tend to miss appointments to call the practice back to confirm they received the message and that they plan to show up.

- Practices should be familiar with the federal Telephone Consumer Protection Act. This law, while initially intended to prevent unwanted calls from telemarketers and autodialing services, does have ramifications for any business reaching out to patients, clients or other contacts via phone or text.

  ○ Make sure you conduct a comprehensive background check of any service you might hire to make automated phone appointment confirmations for your practice. It's also a good idea to find out whether any of your colleagues use that service and what their experiences have been. As you know, word-of-mouth remains one of the best ways to find reliable, reputable service providers.

Ask patients to consent to the **method of contact** they prefer and make a note to handle all future appointment reminders that way.

Managing Patients

Patient Satisfaction Surveys

Many dental practices find it helpful to survey patients about their experience. Questions can range from how comfortable the reception area is to how long they waited to receive treatment and whether they felt their dental concerns were adequately addressed.

- Customize your surveys so they're appropriate to the patient's experience. For instance, a new patient should be asked different questions than a patient who came in for a routine cleaning.

- Be realistic about how many questions you include in the survey. Don't ask questions that aren't relevant or that don't provide valuable input. Remember that patients who complete the survey are using their personal time to provide feedback.

- Ask the most important questions first so you receive the most valuable information even if the patient doesn't complete the entire survey.

- Make sure the emails and surveys give patients a way to opt out of future communications.

- Your practice management software may include an electronic instant survey for patients. Make sure you review the questions asked to ensure they're relevant to your practice and your patients.

- Several online survey vendors allow you to create a free, customized survey that can be shared with patients via email so they can complete it anonymously. While this option requires some investment of staff time, it allows for complete customization of questions and possible responses. Keep in mind that basic surveys are generally free and that lengthier questionnaires, or in-depth reporting of results, typically involve additional costs. Determine whether the vendor who fields your survey is a HIPAA business associate and, if so, make sure you have the required business associate agreement in place.

- Assign a staff member to compile and share survey results with you and the entire team. Use that information for a team discussion about ways to improve processes, communications, or other areas where change might be helpful.

- Consider inviting satisfied patients to provide post treatment feedback on social media. This can be done at the end of your survey or mentioned by your front desk staff.

    ◦ Positive online reviews are today's version of word-of-mouth advertising and can be an effective way to attract new patients.

Many dental practices find it helpful to **survey** patients about their experience.

Positive online reviews are today's version of word-of-mouth advertising and can be an effective way to attract new patients.

Managing Patients

Resources:

- **Sample Copy for Sending Patients a Satisfaction e-Survey**, p. 56

- **Sample Reminder Message to Increase Patient Survey Response Rate**, p.57

- **Sample Patient Satisfaction Survey**, p.58

Managing Patients

SAMPLE COPY FOR SENDING PATIENTS A SATISFACTION E-SURVEY

Dear [*Insert Patient's Name*]:

To provide the best possible service to meet your dental care needs, we would appreciate feedback on your experience in our dental office.

Please take a moment within the next week to complete this brief e-survey about your most recent visit to our practice.

Thank you for your valuable input.

Sincerely,

Dentist Name

If the email includes commercial content, such as advertising or a message promoting a product or service, comply with the CAN-SPAM Act (for example, CAN-SPAM requires that the email include your physical postal address and instructions for opting out of future emails from you). You must promptly honor any opt out requests.

Managing Patients

SAMPLE REMINDER TO INCREASE PATIENT SURVEY RESPONSE RATE

Please Note: This email should be sent no sooner than one week after the initial message.

Dear [*Insert Patient's Name*]:

We recently sent you a link to an e-survey asking for your opinions about your most recent visit to our dental practice.

If you have already completed the survey, please know that we appreciate your feedback. If you have not had the opportunity to complete the e-survey, we ask that you take a few moments today to let us know your opinions.

Thank you for your valuable input.

Sincerely,

Dentist Name

If the email includes commercial content, such as advertising or a message promoting a product or service, comply with the CAN-SPAM Act (for example, CAN-SPAM requires that the email include your physical postal address and instructions for opting out of future emails from you). You must promptly honor any opt out requests.

Managing Patients

SAMPLE PATIENT SATISFACTION SURVEY

	How did we do? (1= Lowest, 4= Highest)
1. Were you greeted in a prompt friendly manner?	1 2 3 4
2. Was your provider sensitive to your concerns?	1 2 3 4
3. Was your treatment clearly explained?	1 2 3 4
4. Was it easy to schedule an appointment?	1 2 3 4
5. How would you rate your overall experience?	1 2 3 4
6. Would you return to our practice in the future?	1 2 3 4
7. Would you refer a friend or family member to our practice?	1 2 3 4

Patient Relations

Trust and communication are the cornerstone of any successful business. This is especially true in dentistry. As a dentist, you're required to wear multiple hats and to balance being a clinical health care provider with being a CEO. While your focus is primarily on the clinical aspect and the satisfaction you receive from providing quality care, managing a successful dental practice requires more than superior clinical skills. Good patient relations go beyond providing excellent treatment and communication. They include managing all types of situations, both positive and negative. Being ready for any event is the best way to handle the full scope of patient relations.

Clear and open communication with every patient is crucial because it protects both your patients and your practice. Minor details that can have major impact can easily be overlooked unless you've created a formal plan, usually in the form of an office manual that provides consistent, quick and accurate answers to issues that come up frequently.

Reactivation/Retention

Patients stop visiting the dentist for a variety of reasons. Sometimes they postpone appointments because they're not experiencing any dental issues. Use your recall system to identify patients that haven't been seen for a while and then contact them to come in for a check-up.

- Patients often develop good relationships with the hygienist or someone in the front office. Have the staff member who knows the patient best make a personal telephone call to the patient. Have them mention how long it's been since the last appointment and what type of treatment was most recently done. Tell them what was being monitored and why it's important they continue to receive care on a regular basis.

  - Identifying which staff member has the best relationship with each lapsed patient takes effort but that person will probably be able to motivate the patient to make–and keep–an appointment.

  - Consider contacting the patient by phone yourself. Even though your time is tight and your schedule is booked, blocking out a little bit of time each week to make these types of calls is likely to have a lot of impact. This personal contact strengthens the doctor-patient relationship and proves that you genuinely care about the patient's oral health.

Use your **recall system** to identify patients that haven't been seen for a while and then contact them to come in for a check-up.

- Send the patient a follow up letter that describes new services and equipment, introduces new team members and shares any other practice news that makes it enticing to come back.

- Accept that it's time to let go of patients who fail to respond to repeated attempts to make contact. Write one last letter that lets them know they're overdue for an appointment and that their oral health could be at risk because of the time that's elapsed between visits. Remind them about the links between oral health and overall health. Give them a deadline for responding before placing the patient in the inactive category. Make notes in the patient's chart that document your efforts to encourage them to return to the practice.

- Keeping patients active takes time and effort that will be rewarded with a hygiene schedule that has very few openings. If necessary, consider hiring an additional staff person, even on a part-time basis, to assist in the process.

Resources:

- **Sample Reactivation Phone Scripts and Reactivation Letter**, p.61-62
- **Tips for Customizing the "What's New" Reactivation Letter**, p.63
- **Sample Patient Reactivation Letters**, p.64

Keeping patients active takes time and effort that will be rewarded with a hygiene schedule that has very few openings.

Noncompliance

Certain patients simply won't brush, floss or follow even the most basic home care instructions. While cases like these are challenging for your entire staff, a little extra compassion and understanding may have an impact.

- Help patients understand why it's in their own best interest to practice good oral hygiene. One way to start the conversation is to mention news stories about recent research that link good systemic health to good oral health.

- Make sure that you and your team are caring but firm when giving instructions. Do more than simply suggest that patients floss; tell them to floss because they have chronic inflammation. Show them how to floss properly and consider asking patients to demonstrate flossing so staff can ensure they're using the proper technique.

- Noncompliance should be documented in the patient record.

Managing Patients

SAMPLE PATIENT REACTIVATION PHONE SCRIPTS

The Telephone Consumer Protection Act may require you to have specific written consent before calling a lapsed patient to encourage them to make an appointment. In addition, if 18 months or longer have elapsed since the patient last kept an appointment or sent a payment, the Telephone Sales Rule (TSR) may require you to take certain steps such as checking the national do-not-call registry before making the call. Even if 18 months have not elapsed, or the patient is not on the DNC registry, the TSR may prohibit calling patients who have asked you not to call them.

▸ **USE THIS SAMPLE PHONE SCRIPT TO REACTIVATE A LAPSED PATIENT:**

Front Desk Staff: "Good morning, Ms. Doe, this is Jane from Dr. Cooks' office. We recently reviewed our records and see you haven't been to see Dr. Cook since [*insert date*]. If you wish to remain active in our patient files, please call us at [*insert phone number*] to schedule a continuing care appointment. Thank you."

▸ **USE THIS SAMPLE PHONE SCRIPT TO REACTIVATE A PATIENT FOR RECARE:**

Front Desk Staff: "Good morning, Ms. Doe, this is Jane from Dr. Cooks' office. Dr. Cook is very concerned that you are overdue for your continuing care at our practice. It has been over a year since we have seen you. We have an appointment available on Tuesday morning or Thursday afternoon; which of those times work best for you?"

SAMPLE LETTER TO REACTIVATE A LAPSED PATIENT

Practice Letterhead

Date

Dear [*Patient*],

Recently, in the process of reviewing our records, we see that your most recent appointment was [*insert date*].

Since we know how important your oral health is to you, we urge you to call us right away to schedule a continuing care appointment.

For your convenience, the office is open from [*specify hours*]. You can also schedule an appointment online on our website [*list website address*].

Thank you,

Dentist

TIPS FOR CUSTOMIZING THE "WHAT'S NEW" REACTIVATION LETTER

Patient reactivation letters can be written from many points of view, but what often proves effective is one that emphasizes new services or technology in your practice that will help each patient achieve optimal oral health and a dazzling smile.

Today's patients have higher expectations than ever, and are more sophisticated. Showcasing what's new in your practice boosts their confidence in you and your team and reminds them that good oral health-and a bright smile-can help improve their own appearance and confidence.

- Take stock of your practice and make a list of new services, techniques and equipment, as well as any recent continuing education that you and your team have taken and how it will benefit the patient.

- Consider offering an incentive to entice patients to come back, but first evaluate the legal aspects of the incentive. Tricky areas include (a) government payers, (b) sweepstakes/raffles, and (c) usual and customary fees.

- Include information about cosmetic dentistry and other services that can improve the patient's smile. Underscore that message with a little philosophy on how important a dazzling smile is to overall well-being and confidence, especially in the workplace.

- The tone of the letter should be casual and conversational.

- Include visual elements, but avoid using any images that depict unpleasant or graphic dental situations. Pictures that evoke positive images or situations are especially appealing. Make sure that you have appropriate releases and/or permissions in place before using any photos.

Managing Patients

SAMPLE PATIENT REACTIVATION LETTERS

Dear [*insert patient's first name*]:

It's been [*insert time frame*] since we've seen you and we're concerned about your oral health. As we said when you were last here, the status of your oral health may impact your overall health.

▶ **USE THIS LANGUAGE IF THE PATIENT HAD ACTIVE PERIODONTAL DISEASE WHEN YOU LAST SAW HIM OR HER:**

When we last saw you, we had [*begun/discussed*] a treatment plan to bring your periodontal disease under control. You may remember that we talked about how untreated periodontal disease worsens over time and can damage the gums and even the bone that supports your teeth. In fact, periodontal disease is the main reason that people over age 35 lose their teeth.

Please call us today at [*insert phone number*] to set up an appointment. We have many techniques and treatments that can treat periodontal disease. [*Insert name of doctor*] would be happy to discuss them with you and to schedule you for an appointment as soon as possible.

▶ **USE THIS LANGUAGE IF THE PATIENT NEEDS TO REESTABLISH A REGULAR SCHEDULE OF HYGIENE AND ORAL EXAM APPOINTMENTS:**

Our records show that you haven't been in for an oral exam or cleaning since [*insert date of last appointment*]. We're concerned about your oral health and want to remind you that regular dental visits are important part of maintaining your oral, and overall, health.

I recall that you and all of us at [*insert practice name*] have talked about how regular professional hygiene visits–along with daily home care-can help prevent cavities and periodontal disease. With our new [*describe equipment in layman's terms*], your cleaning will be more effective and more comfortable than ever.

You may remember that our oral exams also include an oral cancer screening, which we believe is an important service to provide to each patient. We are committed to working with you to improve your oral health. We've also [*in layman's terms, highlight any new services or equipment that is appropriate or mention additional training that you or your staff has received*] and this offers us new ways to help improve and maintain your oral health.

Please call us today at [*insert phone number*] to set up an appointment. [*Insert name of receptionist*] or another member of the team would be happy to talk with you about what's new in the practice and to schedule you for an appointment as soon as possible.

▶ **USE THIS LANGUAGE IF THE PATIENT PREVIOUSLY EXPRESSED INTEREST IN COSMETIC SERVICES:**

Since you had expressed interest in procedures to improve your smile, I'm happy to tell you that we've added [*in layman's terms, describe an appropriate treatment or technology*].

Please call us today at [*insert phone number*] so [*insert name of receptionist*] or another member of the team can talk with you about this service and other options. She can even schedule you for an appointment so you can learn more about it or have it scheduled at a time that works for you.

▶ **USE THIS LANGUAGE IF IT'S YOUR FINAL ATTEMPT TO CONTACT THE PATIENT:**

Our practice has not seen you in quite a while and we're contacting you to let you know that we're concerned about your oral health.

While we've reached out several times, we have not heard back from you. Please call us at [*insert phone number*] and speak with [*insert name of team member*] so she can schedule an appointment for you to come in for an exam.

Unfortunately, if we do not hear from you by [*insert date, perhaps one month from the date of the letter*], your records will be shifted to inactive status. We would like to have you back in in our practice and hope you'll contact us soon.

Please let us know if you're being seen at another dental practice. We'd also be interested to know what prompted you to seek care somewhere else; perhaps your information will help us identify an opportunity to improve our service.

All of us at [*insert practice name*] wish you the well and hope that you continue to schedule regular preventive dental visits.

Complaints

While patients generally have a high regard for health care practitioners, especially dentists, all dentists have dissatisfied patients at some point in their careers. How you handle this type of situation can strengthen a relationship or indicate that it's time to part ways.

- Remember that a patient complaint does not indicate that you're a bad dentist or that your ability to care for patients is lacking. Typically, patient complaints result from a breakdown in or lack of communication.

- Problems can occur even in the best dentist-patient relationship. When that happens, be open and willing to discuss the patient's complaints or concerns. That genuine dialogue is often all it takes to clear up the matter.

- Patients with complaints usually want the opportunity to be heard, to let off steam, or to get an explanation for why something happened. Maybe they just want an apology, or some type of remedial action and redress that seems appropriate to them. Sometimes they just want to be acknowledged and taken seriously, to be given enough time to fully explain their concern, and to feel as though they're being dealt with honestly and with complete attention.

- Research has found that dentists with the fewest complaints spend more time with each patient at each visit, get to know their patients well, listen actively, maintain a warm and friendly atmosphere, and are humorous, with a warm personality.

Typically, patient complaints result from a **breakdown in or lack of communication**.

Managing Patients

Refunds and Discounts

It's up to you to determine if and when a patient should be given a refund for service provided. Some dentists follow the philosophy that the patient is always right. Others might honor a request for a refund because it's easier than trying to convince the patient that the care provided was appropriate and that the patient was aware of the potential risks. Ultimately, each decision regarding refund requests is based on a number of factors and will vary depending upon the circumstances and, sometimes, will depend upon the patient involved.

- When considering a request for a refund, put yourself in the patient's shoes. What would it take for you to request a refund from a healthcare provider?

  - Sometimes, it's not a matter of money but an issue related to poor communication. Maybe the patient would be satisfied with an attentive ear, an apology, a more detailed explanation, or the promise to provide more information earlier in the process.

- Some dentists also take into consideration their personal feelings about the dissatisfied patient. Are they generally a reliable, dependable patient? Are they a nice person? While that might sound unprofessional, it's human nature to consider such things. Many dentists find it easier to give a refund to a patient who has been a pleasure to treat rather than to one who has been noncompliant and unappreciative.

- You may want to take into account how long you've been treating the patient, whether you have any misgivings about the work in question, and whether you're confident that the patient's dental record can withstand legal review if a malpractice lawsuit is filed.

- If you do agree to provide a refund, have the patient sign a release or fee waiver form. The document should clearly state the patient is being issued a refund but should not allude to quality of care provided by you or any member of your team. That properly prepared and signed document prevents the patient from being able to successfully pursue any future lawsuit in the matter. Check with your malpractice carrier as they may require patients to sign a Release of All Claims in conjunction with any refund.

- If the patient requests a refund because a better and cheaper treatment option should have been used, it's up to you to decide how to proceed. Your response may vary depending on how long you've been treating that

It's up to you to determine if and when a patient should be given a **refund for service** provided.

You may want to take into account how long you've been treating the patient.

Managing Patients

individual. While you may believe that some patients might be satisfied with a simple apology, make sure that you're familiar with any state law that might apply. Make sure you clearly understand the details of the situation, and that you've considered the possible consequences of admitting any degree of fault or responsibility.

- Check with your personal attorney and malpractice carrier for more information about the possible legal ramifications of any apologies or similar statements made to patients and others.

- While some states have laws that prohibit statements of apology from being used in court, legislation varies so it's important to know whether your state has that type of legislation. Some states that prohibit the use of apologies in court enacted those laws on the theory that an apology can enhance patient/provider communications and resolve claims without litigation.

- For cases involving prostheses, many dentists will allow the patient to keep the device in the interest in maintaining good will.

- Remember that you may have to report settlements, refunds or similar payments made to patients to the National Practitioner's Data Bank (NPDB). A written demand claiming malpractice, and payment made through the practice's account, may trigger the requirement to report. This may not be the case if the payment is made through your personal funds. Check with your attorney or malpractice carrier for their advice on when a report must be made, what needs to be included in the report, and any filing deadlines.

Resources:

- **National Practitioner Data Bank Website**
  http://www.npdb.hrsa.gov/guidebook/EMMPR.jsp

Check with your personal attorney and malpractice carrier for more information about the **possible legal ramifications** of any apologies or similar statements made to patients and others.

Managing Patients

Patient Dismissal

Sometimes it's best for a dentist and patient to part ways. In these cases, this is because there's some friction that can't be resolved or a difference in philosophies of care.

- The dentist has the right to dismiss a patient in situations where it is impossible to resolve differences or if the dentist cannot abide the patient's behavior within the practice, as long as the dismissal is not for a legally impermissible discriminatory reason.

- Consult the appropriate state laws and your state dental practice act to determine any requirements about dismissing a patient, including how many days you need to be available to that patient in case of an emergency.

- Handle every patient dismissal cordially and professionally. It should never become personal.

- Develop a template for a dismissal letter. Fill in the details about the cause for the release objectively and advise the patient of the need to find another provider. Also detail the number of days you will be available to treat the patient in the event of an emergency.

- Conduct regular audits of patient records to determine whether problem patients are seen on a regular basis.

- While you should document all communications with patients, including phone calls, it's especially important that you do this when dismissing a patient. That type of information, while considered a best practice in any situation, can be especially helpful in dismissal cases that can become emotionally charged.

Resources:

- **Sample Patient Dismissal Letters**, p.70-71

Sometimes it's best for a dentist and patient to part ways. In these cases, this is because there's some friction that can't be resolved or a difference in philosophies of care.

SAMPLE PATIENT DISMISSAL LETTER

Practice Letterhead

Date

Dear [*Patient*],

It's been [*insert time frame*] since we've seen you and we're concerned about your oral health.

We've reached out several times to remind you that maintaining your oral health is important. We have not heard back from you. Please call us at [*insert phone number*] and speak with [*insert name of team member*] so she can schedule an appointment for you to come in for a thorough exam.

Unfortunately, if we do not hear from you by [insert date, perhaps one month from the date of the letter], your records will be shifted to inactive status. We would like to have you back in our practice and hope you'll contact us soon.

Please let us know if you're being seen at another dental practice. We'd also be interested to know what prompted you to seek care somewhere else; perhaps your information will help us identify an opportunity to improve our service.

All of us at [insert practice name] wish you the well and hope that you continue to schedule regular preventive dental visits.

Sincerely,

CC Patient File

SAMPLE PATIENT DISMISSAL LETTER

Practice Letterhead

Date

Dear [*Patient*],

We have contacted you on several occasions with monthly statements, telephone messages and a personal letter concerning your outstanding balance with our practice. We have determined that, due to your noncompliance with our practice's financial policy, we must terminate our dentist-patient relationship.

In order to allow you adequate time to find another dentist, we will be available for the next thirty days for emergency treatment only. If you need assistance in finding another dentist, you may contact the local dental society at _____ or utilize other resources (e.g. the Internet).

We will forward a copy of your dental records to you or your new dentist upon receiving a signed written authorization request. Please clearly indicate whom you wish to receive a copy and where you wish us to send the records. Please allow five business days from receipt of your request for duplication and mailing.

Sincerely,

CC Patient File

Peer Review

Peer review is an effective, efficient, expeditious, and credible dispute resolution process that benefits both the patient and the provider.

- Peer review involves the convening of a special committee of volunteer dentists from the state or local dental society who review the facts of the case and reach a decision. It is, essentially, an alternative dispute resolution that allows a dentist's decisions and actions to be evaluated by a jury of his or her peers.

- Disputes that may be addressed through peer review typically involve appropriateness of care and quality of care.

- The peer review process entails a mediation and a clinical review. Some states may only offer mediation or clinical review. The peer review committee may conduct a clinical examination to determine appropriate action in cases that cannot be resolved via mediation.

- Both the dentist and the patient are expected to comply with the committee's decision. All information regarding the case is kept strictly confidential. Any records obtained from the dental practice involved are returned once the case is closed.

- Peer review decisions that find in favor of the patient may require the dentist involved to provide a refund or waiver.

  - If the disputing parties accept the committee's recommendation regarding a fee adjustment or waiver, make sure that some type of written release form is used to document the exchange. The form generally provides a release for the dentist from any further liability upon returning the stipulated amount of money or canceling the balance due for work completed.

  - The dentist may also be required to redo the dental work, as long as both the patient and dentist are comfortable with that.

  - The peer review committee may recommend that the dentist involved undergo some type of continuing education in order to improve his or her knowledge and skills.

  - Many peer review programs do not support providing compensation for pain and suffering.

The **peer review** process entails a mediation and a clinical review.

- Peer review decisions that find in favor of the dentist will usually require the patient to pay any fees due for treatment provided (if that was the issue being disputed). Patients may also be asked to return a dental appliance, denture or other oral health device to the dentist as part of the agreement. While the patient is generally asked to accept the committee's findings as the final decision, the dental society has no leverage to enforce the patient's compliance with that request.

Resources:

- **Sample Release Form**, p.75

- **Peer Review in Focus, Dentistry's Dispute Resolution Program, 2013**
  http://www.ada.org/~/media/ADA/Member%20Center/Flles/Peer_Review_Manual_New.ashx

Managing Patients

SAMPLE FEE WAIVER RELEASE FORM

Your malpractice carrier may be able to provide a form that works in your state.

In addition, you may wish to review the <u>Refunds and Discounts</u> section of the *Guidelines for Practice Success™ on Managing Patients* for information regarding reporting refunds resulting from peer review cases to the National Practitioner Data Bank.

RELEASE

I, _____ (hereinafter the patient) for the sum of dollars $ _____ paid to me on this date by _____ [*name of dentist and/or professional corporation*], the receipt of which is hereby acknowledged, fully release _____ [*name of dentist*], _____ [*dentist's professional corporation or business entity, if any*], [*his, her, its, and/or their*] partners, associates, staff, employees and agents, and _____ [*name of released party's insurer*] (hereinafter the released party or parties) from any liability or claims of whatever nature, known or unknown, including, without limitation, claims for personal injury and disability, pain, suffering, mental anguish, loss of income and _____

_____

arising from dental treatment provided to me by released party or parties, including without limitation:

_____

_____

[*describe treatment dates, procedures, surgeries (if any), complications (if any), and dates of those complications*].

[*Optional paragraph*]: I understand that this release shall bind me and my heirs, legal representatives and assigns, and that it shall inure to the benefit of the released party or parties, and to [*his, her its and/or their*] heirs, legal representatives, successors and assigns.

I understand that the receipt of this payment constitutes a final and full release and settlement of any claim I might have against the released party or parties. I also understand that the payment made is not to be construed as an admission of liability on the part of the party or parties hereby released by whom liability is expressly denied. I have read this release, understand the terms used in it and their legal significance, and have executed it voluntarily.

CAUTION: THIS IS A RELEASE – READ BEFORE SIGNING

Patient: _____   Witness: _____

Date: _____

Special Considerations

While every practitioner should be aware of particular considerations that might apply to special needs patients, all patients deserve special considerations that recognize their level of oral health literacy, medical/health issues, possible dental anxiety and other factors.

- Age, culture, language, economic status, values, beliefs and past dental experiences are just a few of the factors that can impact how a patient needs to be treated and motivated to manage appropriate home care.

- You and your staff need to be aware of and sensitive to patients' special concerns. Is it a first dental visit for a pediatric patient? An emergency radiograph for a pregnant patient? Are you seating a geriatric patient with limited mobility? While each situation requires a different protocol, they share the need for you and your staff to be aware of and sensitive to their need for accommodations.

- Many patients with physical or developmental special needs can be treated within the practice with reasonable accommodations. The answers to the following questions can help you determine what changes might be needed to make your practice a better environment for special needs patients:

You and your staff need to be aware of and sensitive to **patients' special concerns**.

  ○ Has your practice met its obligations under the Americans with Disabilities Act (AwDA) and state and local laws?

  ○ Is it possible to implement a plan that, over the course of a few brief visits, familiarizes the patient with the stimuli and environment common

  ○ Can light and sound levels be adjusted to accommodate patients with sensory issues?

  ○ Can family members or caregivers assist the patient in practicing daily tooth brushing at home? Is your staff able to instruct caregivers in proper technique to avoid any injury?

  ○ Can the patient watch as a family member receives treatment so they see what happens and observe desirable patient behaviors?

  ○ Do members of the dental team have training or experience in transferring limited mobility patients to the dental chair?

- Is the dental team familiar with the oral health problems faced by people with disabilities?

- Does the office have mouth props or supportive devices to aid patients who may have difficulties in opening their mouths?

- Are members of the team trained to create personalized oral hygiene programs appropriate to the patient's level of understanding and ability?

- Is the dental health team knowledgeable about assistive devices to help special needs patients perform good home care?

Having a **complete, accurate and current medical history** is absolutely critical when treating patients with special needs.

- While a complete, accurate and current medical history is important for every patient, having that information is absolutely critical when treating patients with special needs. A patient assessment form can help identify any special techniques or accommodations that might make treatment a more positive experience for the special needs patient.

  - The patient assessment form should detail the nature of the disability, the degree of the patient's independence, dental history, social history, communication ability (vision or hearing loss), transportation needs and preferred appointment times.